Letters to Little Rock

Letters to Little Rock

Poems by

Jennifer Horne

© 2024 Jennifer Horne. All rights reserved.
This material may not be reproduced in any form, published,
reprinted, recorded, performed, broadcast,
rewritten, or redistributed without
the explicit permission of Jennifer Horne.
All such actions are strictly prohibited by law.

Cover design by Shay Culligan
Cover image courtesy of Jennifer Horne
Author photo with her father by Rhonda Barton

ISBN: 978-1-63980-631-7
Library of Congress Control Number: 2024943765

Kelsay Books
502 South 1040 East, A-119
American Fork, Utah 84003
Kelsaybooks.com

For my sister, Mary Thach Horne

Acknowledgments

For "Questionnaire for the Death of a Loved One," I wish to thank Martha Dallas, Vermont Celebrants, LLC, on whose questionnaire this is based, and Glee Noble for sharing it with me.

Thanks to my "writing buddies," Rachel Dobson and Wendy Reed, for reading these poems in their early stages, and especially to Wendy for her suggestion that I could try using form as a way to approach this material. Without that suggestion, this book would not have found its present shape. Thanks also to Lenoir-Rhyne University, where I worked on some of the poems during my time there as writer-in-residence, and thanks to Rand Brandes for inviting me to LRU and Beth Brandes for her compassion and insight in reading and responding to some of the poems.

Thanks to these publications for including my poems:

All Night, All Day: Life, Death, and Angels, edited by Susan Cushman, Madville Publishing: "A Thing or Two," "Lines," "Playing Hooky," "Tears," "The Messages"
Decade: 10 Years of Poetry and Barbecue, the Laura (Riding) Jackson Foundation: "Traveling Back to Little Rock"
Eastern Structures: "Time, Passing"
Father (Gritty Southern Fatherhood Anthology), Bluewater Publications: "Hot Springs High," "Nomenclature"
The Orchards Poetry Journal: "Look Forward To"
The Southern Poetry Anthology, Vol. X: Alabama from Texas Review Press: "College Tour"
What Things Cost: an anthology for the people, a fundraiser for the Poor People's Campaign, edited by Rebecca Gayle Howell and Ashley M. Jones, with Emily Jalloul: "The Horns of Horns Valley Moved from Alabama to Arkansas, Gained an 'e,' and I Returned Three Generations Later for Graduate School in Creative Writing, of All Things"
I wish to thank Ashley Jones for asking me to contribute to the anthology; her request inspired this poem.

Notes on the photo on the back cover:

The photo of the author's father, circa 1940, was probably taken at the Mena, Arkansas train depot, standing next to the Kansas City Southern Railway (KCS) Southern Belle passenger train. This is the only surviving photograph of him as a boy.

Contents

Questionnaire for the Death of a Loved One	15
March	18

I. A Deciduous World

Lines	21
Hold	23
At Your Funeral	25
Liquid Bandage	26
I can see the leaves on the trees	27
Tears	29
1:30 Sunday Blues	30
The Messages	31
The Way	32
Playing Hooky	33
Time, Passing	34

II. Windows and Stories

Things I Can't Look Up	37
Windows	38
The Rain Story	40
The Honky-Tonk Story	41
The Swimming Story	42
The Aspirin Story	43
The Blackboard Story	44
The Pink Sheet Story	45
The Bully Story	46
The Store Story	47
The Motorbike Story	48
The Sandstorm Story	49
The Pilot Story	51
The Cigarette Story	52

III. Clutch

After Yardwork	55
The State Fair	56
Coach	58
Clutch	59
Hilton Head Vacation	62
College Tour	63
WhoWhatWhenWhereWhyHow	64
57 Years Old	65

IV. Look Forward To

Nomenclature	69
Look Forward To	71
Smalls	72
Hot Springs High	73
Fresh Market Reuben	74
A Good Life	75
A Party the Likes of Which	76
A Thing or Two	77
The Horns of Horns Valley Moved from Alabama to Arkansas, Gained an "e," and I Returned Three Generations Later for Graduate School in Creative Writing, of All Things	78
Traveling Back to Little Rock	85

Me: "What's so funny?"
You: "I just told myself a joke I hadn't heard before."

Questionnaire for the Death of a Loved One

Your name: Jennifer Horne

Relationship to the deceased: Daughter

Full name of the deceased: Allan Wade Horne

Today's date: January 21, 2018

Deceased's nicknames or family names: Born Allan Wade Horne, he was nicknamed "Dick" by his seven older brothers and sisters, and was called Dickie as a child. For his adult nicknames, please see "Nomenclature"

Stories from his early life: Please see "The Rain Story," "The Honky-Tonk Story," "The Swimming Story," "The Aspirin Story," "The Blackboard Story," "The Pink Sheet Story," "The Bully Story," "The Store Story," "The Motorbike Story," "The Sandstorm Story," and "The Pilot Story"

Stories from his middle life: Please see "The Cigarette Story," "The State Fair," "Clutch," and "WhoWhatWhenWhereWhyHow"

Stories from the latter part of his life: Please see "57 Years Old" and "Time, Passing"

What do you want to tell the world about your loved one? Please see "Things I Can't Look Up," "Hold," and "Smalls"

What was your loved one passionate about in life? Was there a motto or philosophy that he lived by? Please see "Look Forward To"

What did the person do to contribute to the world? Please see "Windows"

What did he teach you about life? Did your loved one have any memorable quotes or sayings? Please see "Liquid Bandage" and "I can see the leaves on the trees"

Did your loved one ever do anything that was random, quirky, and charming? Please see "Tears"

What kind of sacrifices did your loved one make? Please see "College Tour" and "Hilton Head Vacation"

How were your loved one's morals and values illustrated in his daily life? Please see "Nomenclature"

How did their life/values shape yours? Please see "The Horns of Horns Valley Moved from Alabama to Arkansas, Gained an 'e,' and I Returned Three Generations Later for Graduate School in Creative Writing, of All Things"

Where did the person show commitment and perseverance? Please see "The Swimming Story"

Do you have any funny stories? Please see "The Pink Sheet Story" and "After Yardwork"

Do you have any teaching stories? Please see "Lines"

What places did the person visit? Please see "Playing Hooky"

Any favorite music, authors, activities, foods, colors, etc.? Please see "The Way"

What was one of his greatest joys? Please see "A Good Life"

What was one of his greatest heartaches? Please see "A Good Life"

What did he find sacred? Did he have any solid beliefs? Please see "The Messages" and "A Thing or Two"

Almost every human has rituals. What things did your loved one do on a regular basis? Please see "1:30 Sunday Blues" and "Fresh Market Reuben"

What positive reactions did other people have toward this person? Please see "A Party the Likes of Which"

Every person changes the world—even if it's in the smallest way. How has your loved one changed the world? Please see "Hot Springs High"

Something you absolutely want to avoid in the ceremony: Please see "At Your Funeral"

Something you MUST have in the ceremony: Peppermints

March

These mourning doves keep following me around
past blushing vines that promise bloom too early
though robins sing and shoots poke green through snow.
I write this poem, step by step, daily.

Oh mourning doves, oh mourning doves, so sleek
in gray attire, what do you want to ask?
I'll tell you how I do the work of grief:
I carve his name into the wooden desk.

I. A Deciduous World

Lines

In North Carolina, my neighbors
had a red phone booth in their yard
amongst the camellias,
rhododendron, hellebores.
The British kind, enclosed
like a many-windowed room,
with TELEPHONE at the top, the kind
I used to stand in every Sunday
when I called from my year abroad in Oxford
and sometimes cried with homesickness.

When you were dying in Arkansas
and I was off teaching in Carolina,
it was snowing hard, and dark,
and I couldn't get to the phone booth.
I'd found an old phone in a closet.
I picked up the heavy receiver,
put my finger in a numbered circle
and dialed, 664-3608, thinking if you
were anywhere reachable, it would be
at the number I'd memorized at age 6,
going off to first grade.

I told you what a good father you'd been,
wished you peace and freedom from pain.
I told you it was OK to go, the way you told me
I could spend a year away from home
in a country you'd never seen
among people you'd never met
because you trusted I would find my way,
because you knew I needed to go,
because although you didn't like yard work
you were a natural gardener, always
encouraging me in the direction of growth.

What lines still connect us—
invisible and taut—beyond
the red box, the squat black phone,
the slim silver magic you learned?
Without a grave to visit, I walked
the local cemetery, spoke
to any stone that spoke to me.
Once—I swear it—I found
golf clubs on a grave, and thought
to speak of it next time you called.

Hold

when you ac-
cidentally
let me step
inside the
houseboat with-
out telling
me the hold
doors were o-
pen to dry
out the hold

        and I stepped
        into air
        falling in-
        to darkness
        flailing for
        a grip, some-
        thing to grab
        onto, you
        felt so guil-
        ty but I
        wasn't ang-
        ry it was
        only a
        mistake like

                when you died
                and you were-
                n't supposed
                to you were
                going to
                get better,

I was go-
ing to come
see you, we
were going
to hold each
other in
a father-
daughter hug,
your sweet skin-
ny old frame
welcoming
me home it's

    like stepping
    into dark-
    ness grabbing
    handfuls of
    air thinking
    what can I
    hold onto

        as I fall

        as I fall

        as I fall

At Your Funeral

You were a "ding dong daddy from Dumas," I heard the minister say.
Had I missed an essential fact of your life? My memory recoiled.
I reckon you all don't know me at all. I just got here today.

My face got flushed and my chest grew tight and I didn't want to stay.
Walking out would cause a scene. Remaining felt disloyal.
You were a ding dong daddy from Dumas, I heard the minister say.

I knew you were never from Dumas. You were hill country, all the way.
The flat lands of the delta were not your native soil.
I reckon you all don't know me at all. I just got here today.

Should I stand and interrupt him? What was the proper play?
The poor man got his facts mixed up, but nothing true was spoiled.
You were a ding dong daddy from Dumas, I heard the minister say.

Oh, Daddy, I went back and forth. But it ended. Time to pray.
In the quiet and the dark I heard you remark, "Honey, don't get
    embroiled."
I reckon you all don't know me at all. I just got here today.

I could almost hear you laughing: "Guess what happened? Hey,
at my very own funeral service, clear as water that's been boiled,
'He was a ding dong daddy from Dumas,' I heard the minister say."
I reckon you all don't know me at all. I just got here today.

Liquid Bandage

That little brown bottle in
my medicine cabinet
I bought because you
enthused about how
invisibly it covers
nicks and scrapes
while the body darns itself
back to wholeness.
Every inch of me feels
tender, skin too thin.
Let's make a joke:
I may need more
than one bottle.

I can see the leaves on the trees

is what we both said when we got glasses,
decades apart, in a green season.

Home after your funeral, I kick
the dry leaves in my yard. I should rake.

In the bad night of the dream of your death,
I am always driving across Mississippi

through winter-bare trees,
clouds scudding like calved icebergs.

Fifty years ago when you pointed at
the right field billboard, "Bud's wiser,"

and I, already a good reader,
saw only a blur, you sighed,

knowing I'd inherited not only myopia,
a lifetime of corrective lenses,

but probably, along with attention to detail
brought on by early practice in nearsightedness,

its companion: the ability to imagine
the many ways a situation could go wrong,

useful both in law and writing fiction,
not so much in daily life. We worried.

We live in a deciduous world,
always the letting go.

The falling, the falling,
the chill coming on, the coming of winter,

only later the bone-sharp
hope of visible growth.

Tears

On your last visit,
you left your tears behind.

Four little plastic tubes,
ampoules, you'd call them—

the word sounding old-fashioned,
like the way you signed

your full name
on the card reader,

taking your time
to get it right

though it would quickly disappear.
There, and then not there.

1:30 Sunday Blues

You used to call me every Sunday,
        so we could talk on the telephone.
You'd call every single Sunday,
        we'd talk on the telephone.
Now when I pick up the receiver at 1:30,
        there's nothing but a dead dial tone.

We'd tell each other our weekly stories,
        catching up on all the news.
Oh, we told each other the week's stories,
        caught up on all our news.
Now I don't know where to put those stories,
        that's why I sing these blues.

When the time comes around on Sunday,
        I feel empty as an abandoned school.
When that time comes 'round on Sunday,
        I'm empty as an abandoned school.
I'm going to write you a letter this Sunday,
        though I may feel like a fool.

You used to call me every Sunday,
        so we could talk on the telephone.
You'd call every single Sunday,
        we'd talk on the telephone.
Now when I pick up the receiver at 1:30,
        there's nothing but a dead dial tone.

The Messages

In Ireland, what I call "running errands"
they call "getting the messages."
Along with the ordinary comes the coincidental,
along with the daily, the convivial.
Along with the necessary
may come the serendipitous,
chores not incompatible with connections.
Taking a necessary walk
around the pretty campus
with my alert brown dog,
I watch her sniff socially at a blade of grass,
reading, getting her messages,

stopping stock still to stare at things I can't perceive.

I think maybe I'm willing to believe—
or at least not willing to not believe—that
you might be getting a few messages through.
The week before you died,
calling from the hospital,
you told me we'd see each other soon,
we'd *find a way to get together,*
one way or another.
It's not like you to knock or tap
or blink the lights
or shimmer. But sometimes, not looking,
I still catch the odd, peripheral glimmer.

The Way

you said sal-mon,
        pronouncing the *l*
the way you carefully signed your name
        on the electronic credit card pad
the way you turned your high school ring
        around your finger with your other fingers
the way you shuffled coins in your pocket
        like when you were ten and a newsboy
the way you loved being surprised
        into laughter, a full body laugh
the way you adjusted your glasses on the bridge of your nose
        by grasping the edges, as I do now
the way catfish on Friday night and steak on the grill
        on Saturdays made you happy
the way you'd fold a hundred-dollar bill into fourths
        and slip it to me "for gas money"
the way you cleared your throat so distinctively
        even in a crowd we knew it was you
the way you sometimes called yourself "the Great One,"
        laughing about it, but still proud

Playing Hooky

I thought you were gone. But, remembering the story you told of getting mad at your fourth-grade teacher who punished you for erasing your math problem when you knew she'd said it was okay, I wonder if you're just skipping, the way you skipped the rest of fourth grade, waiting until your mother left to take the bus to her job at the ladies clothing store, watching her from the strip of park on the avenue and then returning home. It was the injustice you felt so keenly, like having to wear the stupid mask when your lungs couldn't do the job on their own. Maybe, I tell myself, you're just playing hooky now, skipping life for a little while, outside somewhere, not in a park but on the golf course, free to walk the cart-paths, dream of your third hole-in-one.

Call me from the airport gate, waiting for your plane home, with your well-worn briefcase and zippered carry-on hanging bag. Call me from the high room of a conference hotel, your voice filled with wonder at the beautiful view. Call me from your office looking over the Arkansas River, the little boy from the Ozarks, the grown man with stacks of case files in a pattern only you understand and a sign next to the disposable coffee cups you plan to reuse:

> "Do Not
> Touch or Remove
> Any Cups In
> This Office
> Thank You—Allan W. Horne."

Time, Passing

When you were leaving, I stayed up late, a death watch.
For comfort, she wore your memory's weight, a death watch.

Only two years and five months later, she followed you.
The time between was mostly a long wait, a death watch.

I sat in the dusk, lit a candle, read a prayer from an old book,
saying goodbye to your love, your mate, a death watch.

So. That part is over. I am surprised. No, bewildered.
Part of me here, part there. You cannot backdate a death watch.

Belongings become another's once we are gone from them.
All things assessed as unneeded don't rate a death watch.

Rooms emptied, a whole house clears like a shriven conscience,
blameless, enormous, passive, the clean slate a death watch.

Horns might announce that those who carry our name have a way
of remaining. To see how we circumnavigate a death, watch.

II. Windows and Stories

Things I Can't Look Up

I can look up the weather
the latest news the gossip.
Like a queen I command
the world's legions of trivia
with my oh so regal hand.

But now
I will never know
exactly how the marriage came apart or rather
why you couldn't put Humpty-Dumpty back together again.

I forget which actor you saw
in the pizzeria in Naples. Anthony Quinn?

I'd like to hear more about your mother.

Please, if you could, tell us all the stories of Hot Springs
one more time, so I won't forget any details.

I never asked what it felt like to be you
when you were young, full-hearted
and mischievous, a gentle boy but stubborn.

The little myriad mysteries are stacking up
and in this age of all facts
I find I am standing
in the middle of the room,
turning, turning,
a blindfolded child in a game
whose rules I'm still learning.

Windows

Your father, older, silent,
prone to drink,
when storms came up

went from window to window
in that rented house
in Caddo Gap,

worry-watching the sky:
a trapped bird
who didn't dare fly.

On the thirty-seventh floor
of the highest downtown building,
your corner office

was all sky.
From there you could see
your father at the windows,

your daily paper route,
the changing sky and endless chop
aboard a Navy ship.

The ship's library fed you.
Each day a new horizon.
You told us how Steinbeck

opened up a view
of the Depression
beyond your Ozark hills.

Far past those early years
you stood at the windows,
Arkansas River below, buildings

you'd name, one by one.
You sorted through stacks
of case files, reflecting, nearly done.

I am telling your stories
looking through my window
into a clear space

where sunlight falls.
Not the far horizon
nor wide river below,

just that sunlit space,
an unworried watching,
seeing what wanders into view.

The Rain Story

We saw the
very place
on the trip
to Caddo
Gap: the gas
station where
it rained on
one side, not
the other.
Step to one
side: rain. Step
again: none.
"This is the
very spot
where I learned
it doesn't
rain in all
places at
the same time!"

The Honky-Tonk Story

"Somebody got
knifed at the
honky-tonk
that used to
be right here.
They asked all
present what
they'd seen, and
one woman"—
you recalled
after all
these years, said
"I didn't
see nothin'.
I was just
addin' to
the crowd." And
"just addin'
to the crowd"
became your
favorite
way to say
not doing
much, just here.

The Swimming Story

"My brothers
took me down
to the lake
to teach me
to swim. They
threw me in
the water,
off the dock.
That was the
lesson." We
gasped, asked if
you came back
up. "I'm here,
aren't I?"

The Aspirin Story

Caddo Gap:
deep in the
Depression.
Someone in
your family
had a bad
headache, but
no money.

By luck, your
brother found
a tin box
in the creek:
aspirin.
That was how
that headache
was treated,

you told us.
Your smile was
ambiguous,
a line drawn,
poverty
or bounty
your point,
maybe both.

The Blackboard Story

That teacher—
the one who
said you could
erase your
work, and then
scolded you
when you did—
became our
enemy,
too, her cold
injustice
the hot slap
on our palms
her wrongness
our lesson
on power.

The Pink Sheet Story

Paper boy
(you) called "pink
sheet, pink sheet!"

The racing
page in Hot
Springs, all the
day's horses!

Paper boy
(you) called "pig
shit, pig shit!"

Someone stopped,
turned his head,
cocked his ear.

"Pink sheet!" you
called, hid your
smile. "Who needs
a pink sheet?"

The Bully Story

A childhood
playground. A
run-of-the-
mill bully.
Your brave boast:
We'll meet you
after school.
"Go, Dickie!"
the boys said
but melted
away when
you turned to
them for help.
"Got my butt
beat pretty
good that day."
Learned you could
only count
on yourself.

The Store Story

Accused of
loitering
over the
comic books,
you vowed, I
will never
enter that
store again.

Your friends, not
taking that
vow, left you
stranded on
the sidewalk,
strong in your
conviction
but alone.

The Motorbike Story

Your little
gang of teens
put motors
on your bikes,
rode all the
way from home,
Hot Springs, to
Little Rock
for a game.
Reckless, full
of yourselves,
you made a
quick retreat
when LR
boys threw rocks
after the
game ended.
City boys.
You showed them.
Became one.

The Sandstorm Story

A boy from
the Ozark
foothills, you
transplanted
yourself to
Lubbock, to
desert brown,
a football
recruit who
earned summer
money for
school. One day
the wind blew,
a man ran
past you. "Get
inside now,"
he yelled. "A
sandstorm is
coming." The
grains eased their
way under
windowsills
and doors like
a scary
movie you'd
watched downtown
as a boy.
The next day
you decided
Texas was
not for you,

took the bus
home, joined
the Navy,
returned for
college on
the G.I.
Bill, never
again lived
out of sight
of green hills,
considered
your escape
a close call.

The Pilot Story

A Navy
mechanic
for planes on
an aircraft
carrier
not far from
Korea,
you watched the
pilot take
off, fail to
rise, pancake
into the
water. You
saw him, through
cockpit glass,
carefully
unbuckle
all his straps
raise the hatch
calmly wait
for rescue.
"Now that was
grace under
pressure, girls!"

The Cigarette Story

A city
judge in night
court, green and
ambitious,
you always
remembered
the man who
looked you in
the eye when
told he was
not allowed
to smoke in
the courtroom.
Holding the
cigarette
in his right
hand, he put
it out in
the palm of
his left. "That
was one tough
S.O.B.,"
you'd say. "I
rethought night
court after
that fellow."

ially called in, it is called a "comet" because of its speed.

III. Clutch

After Yardwork

I tilt my head down and hold my shirt open and sniff
to see if I smell.
I do not.
It is only the sweet sweatiness
of outdoor labor on a spring day
the way you smelled when you came in
from walking the push mower
back and forth
spraying green confetti.

You loved to take off a sweaty shirt
and toss it at one of us,
laughing, wicked,
your chest pale white,
16 again
and not a care
not a care
in the world.

The State Fair

smelled like
fresh mud
buttered popcorn
machine oil

a hint of manure
cotton candy
diesel exhaust
excitement.

You gave us each
five dollars to spend
understanding
with a gambler's heart

how a little risk,
a little waste,
is needed in an
otherwise orderly life.

We held your hand,
we held our mother's,
the world was so big
and we were small

and the crane
behind the glass
whose buckets we
moved with a slippery crank

was fickle:
sometimes
a shiny bracelet, a lighter, a silver horse
sometimes just

a bit of molded plastic,
or worse,
the hollow gulp
of catching air.

Coach

You're in charge,
    you'd say.
Pitch when you're ready.
Take your time,
    you'd say.
Nice and steady.

I still hear
    your words
when I'm presenting.
Early on,
    they took,
life-imprinting.

Deep breath, then
    a pause.
All eyes attending.
From your first
    inhale,
know your ending.

Clutch

The heady smell of baking bread
drifts into the car.
I'm five again,
legs stuck to the back seat,

passing the Wonder Bread bakery,
picking you up
from work downtown,
Mom at the wheel, Mary beside me.

If I am telling someone
the story of my birth,
I describe Mom moving early
to Little Rock, learning the route

from new house to hospital,
just in case. You stayed behind
to finish your last class.
I waited for you.

At sixteen, I learned to drive
Mom's stately old Mercedes.
You liked its solidity, its name,
she liked its vroom.

Maybe I should've learned
on manual transmission.
I couldn't shift, not even
when you bought me the yellow car

for Christmas. We spent the day
lurching across the stadium parking lot,
both of us trying so hard,
getting nowhere. There were tears.

You taught me to ride a bike,
throw a ball, cast a rod,
but there was no teaching me
the dance of gas and clutch.

I stalled so often it became
the day's punctuation mark.
Full stop. Full stop. The silence
so not neutral. The ball dropped.

The next day, you swapped
standard yellow, slightly bruised,
for drivable lime green
at my uncle's small-town lot.

My shame: I complained
about the color. You remember.
And you knew I'd shift gears,
metaphorically, at least.

Decades beyond that day,
in automatic optimism, I turn
the dial on your old transistor radio,
the one you shaved by.

Static. Distant voices
the red line catches on.
The little black box
wants to keep its secrets.

I try for the just-right touch
that eases into clarity.
If I can get it right,
I can move forward.

Hilton Head Vacation

You were the man, and
the man drives the whole way. How
tired you must have been.

College Tour

I can see you hunched at the steering wheel,
black leather gloves holding tight,
peering ahead, willing the car to stay on the frozen road,

your good wool coat, your checked wool hat
talismans against mishap,
taking me north through the Ozarks

from Little Rock to far-away Missouri
through sudden snow on rollercoaster roads
with unseen drop-offs.

I was quiet so you could concentrate
quiet like both of us reading a book in the same room
but never did I worry you wouldn't get us through.

I knew. I'm driving now, halfway lost
somewhere north of Atlanta, picturing
your steady hands on the wheel:

black gloves, near white-out of snow,
your love expressed in getting me
where you hoped I wouldn't go.

WhoWhatWhenWhereWhyHow

How old was I? 21?
When you moved out.
Not your choice.

How old were you? Newly 50?
When you asked me
to help the movers.

How old was the crack
in the marriage
that finally went Richter?

How did I know
in childhood nightmares
to fear it?

How did you stand
the first night
alone in a rented apartment?

What made you think
I was ready to handle
the men who came with the truck
and all they dismantled?

57 Years Old

and I'm hiding
our late-night
downtown bar trip
from you

scrubbing smoke
out of my hair
before meeting
for breakfast

so you don't
worry retroactively
about what
could have happened

but didn't.

IV. Look Forward To

Nomenclature

As a boy, you picked peaches.
Had enough of outdoor work.
No gardener, you developed
your own plant naming system
based on color:
yellalias,
purpulias,
blueinnias,
oranganias.

Law school Latin
might have schooled you
for genus, species,
Linnaean nomenclature, but
you resisted classification.
You had so many names—
Allan, Al, Dick, Coach, Judge—
your self the same beneath each,
easy smile, solid core.

I knew you by another name,
the one that stays. The name we'd call
when you came in the door
from work, putting the day aside
with your hat and briefcase,
letting us shout
our welcomes, our relief
at your reliable reappearance
from the shadow world of work.

Last year, visiting the Bernice Garden,
I saw how you looked at
each flower individually,
studied each piece of outdoor sculpture.
When you thought no one was watching,
you slipped a folded bill
to the man who sat quietly
on a bench next to his cart
and called him Sir.

Look Forward To

Always have something to look forward to,
you'd say, even if it's just a peppermint,
tucked in a jacket pocket. You'd produce
the pinwheeled sweets, leaving a restaurant,

reminding us of pinwheels from the dimestore,
bought with allowance money, shiny quarters,
a way to catch the wind, befriend the hour.
You'd say the treat was in the looking forward

as much as in the crunch or slow dissolve,
a promise to yourself that dullness passes,
that little sparks of dazzle light the path
better than any brilliant, one-time blast.

Smalls

The little hoard shines:
watch, cuff links, money clip, ring.
I will take them home,
and your phone. It holds a charge
still, we learn, as though alive.

Hot Springs High

You wore the ring on your right hand,
the boy from Caddo Gap made good.
You drove us through the old neighborhood.
You'd saved to buy that modest band.

The high school boy was now a man,
ready to live as a man should.
You wore the ring on your right hand.
The boy from Caddo Gap made good.

Now it is mine. Now I can,
in its light heft, feel how it stood
for all you'd done, and all you would.

Turning it idly to ponder, plan,
you wore the ring on your right hand.
The boy from Caddo Gap made good.

Fresh Market Reuben

"Bless their hearts, the peacemakers,
For they shall try to make everyone happy."

You struck up a friendship
with the cheerful deli woman,
learned of her hard life,
the absence of a man,
her postponed plans.

Tipped her every week
for the take-home Sunday Reuben,
a way to show you cared,
make things a bit more even,
help a fellow human.

Weekly, the sandwich grew,
so much corned beef
it made an extra sandwich.
Too much. It gave you grief,
but how to ask the giver for relief?

Remember? You gave up that Sunday habit.
Let the friendship lapse.
Did she wonder why you'd stopped,
imagining you'd moved, perhaps,
or worse? Filling in the gaps.

I don't judge.
I'd easily do the same.
We both want to be kind
and yet, avoiding pain,
our own or others', end up more to blame.

A Good Life

You gave her your heart, your promise of forever. You gave her your dedication to your work, the good provider. You were the father who always showed up, the husband who tried never to give her cause to cry. You gave her the house in the good neighborhood, the nice car, even a pool in the backyard. You mowed the lawn with the push mower and trimmed the hedge with clippers and paid the bills and stayed away from any edge or danger. You did everything right and she made the household work until it didn't work for her anymore. You could never understand because you'd done what you both wanted, you'd made a good life together and what more could she want? Your sister Wanda once told me that when you were first married and driving home from school for Christmas, the car radio broke and the two of you sang all the way from Fayetteville to Hot Springs. How could two people who could do that together ever get divorced, she asked me.

A Party the Likes of Which

The vestigial Irish in you wanted the wake, the grand send-off. Throwing a game is bad; throwing a party is good. Also bad: throwing in the towel, throwing out the baby with the bathwater, throwing up and throwing up your hands. You never give up. When the ball is thrown to you, you watch it into your hands, and you don't get ahead of yourself and try to throw it before you've caught it. That's a story I would have told at your party, how you taught me to throw and catch, and all the girls you ever coached in softball would be there, too, telling how you drove the ones whose families didn't have cars to practices and games, paid for their uniforms, and took everyone out for pizza afterwards. Let's have your golfing buddies, your poker gang, your high school friends, that girl you had a crush on for seventy years. We'll welcome your first wife, the one you let go so reluctantly, and the second, she of the country club years, who shaped her life around yours and guarded your ashes. Let's throw down the gauntlet to death and call your long-gone brothers and sisters, your mother and silent father, all those cousins from Caddo Gap and Talladega. We'll need a larger venue now, because a parade of lifelong clients is coming in, too, and you're not here but still you're at the center of it all, telling yourself a joke you hadn't heard before and laughing, scotch in hand, just throwing it out there to see what sticks, and like stick-me-tights from a walk in the woods, memories of you cling and I keep finding more. Here's your party, and let it go long, let it go all night until dawn. Let's throw caution to the winds and eat and drink and lie and laugh and then tomorrow let's get up late and overthrow our sadness like a dictator whose time has come and must, now or never, be vanquished.

A Thing or Two

I got your message, the one
where you said you had some things
to tell me but there were one
or two barriers in the way, or layers, things
you couldn't quite get through. It's one
time-tested mode to speak through dreams, another thing
entirely to tell me but not tell me. Can anyone
know where the messages come from? A thing
like this, an instance, might lead one
to wonder about the liminal nature of things.
You were smiling but perplexed, like that one
time you tried to learn the computer, a thing
I use now to skip place and time like a stone.
Now I'm thinking, what if your message was just the thing
you told me, and not one blessèd thing more?

The Horns of Horns Valley Moved from Alabama to Arkansas, Gained an "e," and I Returned Three Generations Later for Graduate School in Creative Writing, of All Things

(In Memoriam, Allan Wade Horne, 1932–2018)

You
    the first of 8
        to graduate
high school
    your four brothers
        and three sisters
starting work early
    working hard
        proud
so proud
    of their
        little brother
a little awed later
    when you'd
        done so well

your mamma
    the seamstress
        at the ladies dress shop
your papa
    the timber cruiser
        in the Ozark hills
would walk miles
    to town
        to find the job

brother Bob
    dropped him in the woods
        he couldn't drive

your mamma
    added the "e"
        when another Horn
in Caddo Gap
    kept getting
        her mail
including
    paychecks
        he cashed

Why didn't I understand?
Why didn't you tell me?

we two little girls
    growing up
        so easy
so comfortable
    in our comfort
        we didn't
we couldn't
    you didn't
        want us to see
how it
    had been
        growing up poor
the stories retold
    as triumphs
        over adversity

when someone
    had a headache
        and no money
for medicine
    deep in the hills
        deep in the Depression
you found aspirin
    by the creek
        still in its cellophane packet

the school
    in Hot Springs
        where you moved
from Caddo Gap
    you were eight
        you had to repeat a grade
but later would say
    it was
        the best thing
that could have happened
    you needed
        the extra year

you moved houses often
    you didn't ever
        say why
you had
    a little boy job
        delivering papers
and you sang
    for change
        at the big hotel

when I wanted
    a paper route
        you said no
I loved you
    I would've
        loved you
if you'd said
    how hard
        it was

Why didn't I understand?
Why didn't you show me?

we drove
    to Caddo Gap
        in your Lincoln
your lawyer car
    your cousin
        was there
on the porch
    of the general store
        as though
he'd been
    waiting
        all these years
you marveled
    at where you'd
        come from

I could see
    the ghost
        of a slim, shirtless boy
overall-clad
    barefoot
        playing in the creek
observing his world
    closely through
        nearsighted eyes
so why
    couldn't I see
        that the story
of picking peaches
    the hated
        itch of fuzz
had a sharp pit
    a hard knot
        of need?

Why didn't I understand?
Why didn't you let me?

Magician-father
    your sleight
        of hand
hid the pain
    that old wound
        of shame
misdirection said
    look over here
        at pride

the client
    you most admired
        had a
6th-grade education
    but I
        didn't see
you wore
    the same bootstraps
        as he
success was
    the measure
        of the man
you were
    always going to find
        the way
things finally
    turned out all right
        in the end
when you praised
    his hard work
        why didn't I understand?

Why didn't I understand? Why
didn't I see?

I'm ashamed
    I didn't hold
        those tales
up to the light
    but like an
        illustrated
Bible story
    I saw them
        with a child's eyes
I have so many years
    to go back and
        reappraise
appreciate each bike
    each Christmas
        each trip to the doctor
your gift
    was our ignorance
        your loss
was our taking
    for granted
        this is
the longest
    thank-you note
        in the world dear
Allan
    Wade
        Horne

Traveling Back to Little Rock

The season turns across the delta fields
and fluffs of cotton snow the highway's edge.
This road bisects my world, adult and child,
and, driving north, I think of how I've wedged

myself into a courteous, careful space
where nothing I might say would cause offence.
I smile, recite the things I learned would please,
innocuous, more sensitive than sense.

A scrawl of wintering geese against the clouds
inscribes a path laid out by natural laws,
but I must find my way in flocks of words,
resolve, in fading daylight when I pause
and hear the raucous melody they bring,
to sometimes say the not-expected thing.

About the Author

Jennifer Horne served as the twelfth Poet Laureate of Alabama (2017–2021) and was named the Alabama State Poetry Society's Poet of the Year for 2020. She believes in the power of poetry to connect people, create meaning, bring solace, give joy, and honor mystery.

She is the author of three previous collections of poems, *Bottle Tree* (WordTech Editions, 2010), *Little Wanderer* (Salmon Poetry, 2016), and *Borrowed Light* (Mule on a Ferris Wheel Press, 2019), as well as a collection of short stories, *Tell the World You're a Wildflower* (University of Alabama Press, 2014). She also wrote a biography of the writer Sara Mayfield, *Odyssey of a Wandering Mind: The Strange Tale of Sara Mayfield, Author* (University of Alabama Press, 2024).

Additionally, she has edited a volume of poetry on farming and gardening in the American South, co-edited a collection of short stories by Alabama women, and co-edited three volumes of essays related to southern women, creativity, and spirituality. With her sister, Mary Horne, she edited a posthumous collection of their mother's poetry, *Root & Plant & Bloom: Poems by Dodie Walton Horne* (2020).

Her honors include teaching for a semester as the Visiting Writer-in-Residence at Lenoir-Rhyne University, receiving fellowships from the Alabama State Council on the Arts and the Seaside Institute in Florida, and being awarded the Druid City Literary Arts Award, given by the Tuscaloosa Arts Council.

She has taught creative writing in many settings, including university, elementary and high school, study abroad, conference, and prison classrooms. Raised in Arkansas and a longtime resident of Alabama, she lives in Cottondale, Alabama, with her husband, Don Noble, a literary critic and interviewer.

More about Jennifer can be found online at:
jenhorne.com